she's strong, but she's tired

KT-477-450

other books by r.h. Sin

Whiskey Words & a Shovel

Whiskey Words & a Shovel II

Whiskey Words & a Shovel III

Rest in the Mourning

A Beautiful Composition of Broken

Algedonic

She Felt Like Feeling Nothing

Planting Gardens in Graves

Planting Gardens in Graves II

Planting Gardens in Graves III

Empty Bottles Full of Stories
(with R. M. Drake)

She Just Wants to Forget

Falling Toward the Moon
(with R. M. Drake)

We Hope This Reaches You in Time
(with Samantha King Holmes)

she's strong, but she's tired

r.h. Sin

Andrews McMeel
PUBLISHING®

your intro.

I don't want this for you, that pain you're feeling now. You're anxious to the point of opening this book, and here we are. We always meet this way, don't we? You, tired and weary from loving the wrong person, and me, the stranger who wants nothing but an opportunity to remind you that you matter. And you've given me that chance by deciding to pick up this book, by choosing to let me in. There have been moments when you feel like giving up on yourself, and so you elect to remain in a relationship that is no longer worthy of your energy and time—struggling to smile beneath the weight of your sadness. I may not know you, but I am familiar with the heartache that resides within your heart. I can recall being broken by someone who I thought could care for me. She up and decided to make a mockery of the energy and time I invested, just like he has done to you or maybe she has done to you. No matter the reason for your pain and who may have caused it, you are more than the fucked-up things that have happened to you, and you deserve more than what those fucked-up people gave to you.

It says a lot that you're here. Your eyes scanning this page with a heavy heart and mind that often feels confused and conflicted and tired, overthinking yourself into a corner that makes it difficult to walk away. You're here because you're ready to accept the fact that the person you love is incapable of reciprocating what you've given to them. You're here because the person you've fought for has done nothing but fight you instead of fighting for you. You picked up this book in search of a sign, not knowing that it would appear so early and even though it hurts like hell. The path to heaven on Earth usually begins with walking away from anyone who isn't supporting your idea of what love can be. And I admire you for that. Your ability to recognize your need and desire for more has inspired me to write down these very words. And though I am a bit unaware if these words will reach you in time, at least they're here, scattered upon this page for your eyes to see and for your heart to feel.

May your light shine brighter than it's ever been, despite the darkness that surrounds you, and may your heart pulsate a melody that feels like love, despite you feeling hated by the one you love. May your mind be at ease as you consume these words. I hope you find something here that encourages you to see more of yourself, and once you find more of who you are, I hope you understand more of what you deserve. I hope you never settle again. Because there is wild magic living within your heart, and most of the people you meet will indeed have no clue what to do with it, but I believe you will find the person who will know how to love you correctly. That journey can begin now if you allow it.

---

be here now
be like the sun
you need no permission
to exist, to rise, to shine

be like the moon
make the choice
to light your path
in the depths of darkness

many forms of abuse.

he wants you to allow him back
into the heart he destroyed

he wants you to love him blindly
as if he didn't show you
time and time again
that he was unworthy of your love

he wants you to trust him
with your whole heart
despite knowing that he's betrayed you

breaking a woman down
only to return to her later
is a form of emotional abuse

---

he is not sorry

forgive him

for the sake of yourself

and walk away

for the sake of your future

women are poems

that write themselves

---

it worked for a while

because you were empty

and he was full of beautiful lies

single mothers.

just because you share a child
doesn't give him domain over your life
just because he's the father of your child
doesn't mean you are obligated
to allow him the power to dictate your emotions

there is a way for him to father his child
without compromising your peace of mind

set boundaries, set rules
be the Queen that you are
and demand that he follow
those guidelines

just because you share a child
doesn't mean you have to share yourself
or share in part of his misery

---

precious wild woman

chasing light, chasing love

---

she stopped demanding him
to do all the things he wouldn't do
she stopped begging him to change
and just left him where he stood

Sadly, the world made her feel guilty for wanting to leave a man who could never appreciate her heart. She worried about quitting on someone who gave up on her long ago.

It hurts because you genuinely give a fuck.
Sometimes the heart cares for the wrong person.

The right person will feel like home. So, keep moving until you find a safe place to rest.

You can't lose a man who never deserved to have you.

You can't find safety in the arms of a man who is the reason for your heartache.

the verge of.

How do you bear the heavy weight of sadness as you struggle in silence. Telling others that you're okay while the foundation beneath your house of a heart begins to crumble and sink. You've tried everything, it seems, and none of it works, and so you travel down a road covered in shards of broken hearts, the ones he broke before you even knew him. A history of disappointment, a long list of events that would otherwise be red flags if you had known who he truly was. But he initially gave you the fraudulent version of himself. He made promises to your heart that he was never strong enough to keep, and in the end, all of this made you feel weak. Too tired to walk away but too tired to try again. You're somewhere in the middle of loving him and on the verge of loving yourself enough to leave him behind.

---

an abundance of self-respect
will cause you to detach
from friends who are secretly foes
and family members
who do nothing but harm your heart

the more self-respect you gain
the more willing you are to lose
people who don't deserve
to be kept

high frequency.

It was always his insecurities that made him unfaithful, that and his inability to stand firm in his commitment to the relationship. It takes a great deal of discipline and power to be able to devote oneself fully, and he found difficulty with the idea of remaining true to you. I know it hurts, knowing that the person you love will never be able to reciprocate the energy and care that you've given to them, but it's not a loss for you. Maybe one day he'll look back and wish he had done things differently, or perhaps he'll always be a fool, continually losing the things that should matter most to him. Regardless of what happens, you will go on to love yourself, and someone who matches your frequency will eventually love you.

---

in the end, you realize
you never needed him
he never deserved you
and so his absence
is not a loss

you gain so much more
when you remove people
who don't belong in your life

a concern of mine.

Sometimes I worry about you, the stranger reading these words in this book. The stranger, fighting a war by yourself. It's not easy being you, but you do it to the best of your abilities. It's not easy being you, and yet you survive on nights like this. You inspire me so much, despite being a stranger. You inspire these words as you continue to fight for the love you deserve. I know it feels like moving on is impossible, and sometimes you don't even know where to start, but I hope you know that there is a power that lives within you. A power that no one can destroy. A power that can be used to set yourself free. Sometimes I worry about you, but then I remember how strong you are. I believe in you, and please believe in yourself.

single mothers II.

And to those of you coparenting a child with a man who has been less than kind, create boundaries, rules, guidelines. You deserve to be respected, and he must know that, and he must follow your rule as the Queen you are. You don't have to walk away entirely from him, but you mustn't allow him the power to dictate your life. You are in control. Having a child in common doesn't mean you're obligated to put up with someone's b.s.

Stop giving second chances to fools. Stop providing new opportunities to those who never deserved a chance in the first place.

always this powerful.

Look how far you've come, despite the pain, the heartache. You continue, toward the love you deserve. You've always had this power, but there are nights when you're just tired. Weary from fighting, exhausted from being weighed down by toxic relationships. We may not know each other, but if you're here, you're important, and you matter, and I care, and I will always be here to remind you, to push you, to encourage you. Please, never give in or give up on yourself.

I think you're more than capable of doing what is necessary. No matter how difficult, you hold the required power to set yourself free. I don't want you to hurt anymore, and I hope these words help.

he needs to know.

If you're incapable of being faithful, don't waste her time. If you're too weak to choose her and only her, don't waste her time. If you're not brave enough to love her for all that she is, don't waste her time. She's evolving, and if you can't support and encourage that, don't distract her. Stay out of her way.

---

it is not up to you to keep an unkept man
it is not your job to fight for a man
who is too weak to respect and love you

---

eyes filled with a wild flame
heart ruled by an appetite to love
you went searching for a soul mate
and found more of yourself

---

you who made my soul ache
under the weight of disappointment
and betrayal

you who made me wait for a love
that you were never willing to give

---

he made you cold
then complained
about the weather

---

your ideas of love
molded by people
who pretended to care
molded by individuals
who were only out to use you

your ideas of love
tainted by fools
too weak to appreciate
your presence

dying to live.

and all this time
she was dying to live
and hating herself
for loving the wrong person
who pretended to be right

those days, those nights
fighting an unwinnable war
with an unbeatable foe

telling herself
that if she tried harder
things would change

---

lying to herself
when he refused to be better
blaming herself
claiming that her standards
were too high

lowballing herself
just to keep him in her life

---

i don't think the pain

ever leaves

it lives and lives until you find

the courage to recycle it into strength

---

they're too focused
on your flower
to ever truly appreciate
the strength of your roots

---

where does love really go

when given to the wrong person

coldest summer.

The air is cold in her heart, and ice is being made where she kept her love for you. I think you believed that she would give you another chance, not realizing that she had reached a point of no return. She is changing the locks, boarding up the windows to her soul. No longer willing to play your silly games, no longer willing to pretend to be okay with you crossing lines and tearing into her heart with no regard for what she's feeling. She brought about winter in the middle of summer. She found the courage to freeze you out.

---

you don't win by playing the game
you conquer the players
by ignoring their existence
refusing to give them energy

---

he says nothing when he speaks
there is no meaning behind his words
all those empty promises
and failure to follow through

you've lost so much time
believing in his lies
many years spent on a fool
who had only proven
to be good at being the worst

---

his absence
no longer
made her ache

ready to be alone
willing to be without him

You thought heartache would win, but you survived it.

everything about him was fictional

a made-up character, a genuine fake

---

she misses him

but she wants to forget

You're so distracted by how it ended that you don't even realize how wonderful it is to begin again on your own.

What you tolerate is what they'll continue.to give.

The tiredness in her eyes, in her soul, and in her bones. Loving the wrong person is emotional exhaustion.

I hope you find someone strong enough to be soft with you and your heart.

---

it rains, and this is when you know

the sky is as sad as you are

And you're just trying to be the only one they'll ever love.

Removing people from your life is a symbol of self-respect.

The lowest version of a man is the one who texts "I miss you" while lying in bed with the woman he left you for.

---

one day
her thoughts
will be beautiful
without sadness
and pain
some joy, some peace
and love

---

but you're trying to give your heart

to someone who is only interested in your body

don't

---

it's been years
and time has been unkind to you
your mind has been your biggest enemy
as you are forced to play back
things you wish to forget

i hope you find the peace you deserve

replace him with yourself

you are greater than he is

---

sometimes the hurt is good
some damage becomes wisdom
some pain becomes strength
and you feel broken
but you are stronger than before

---

you need yourself more than you think

you deserve the love you've wasted on others

---

and to think
you sink
because of him
and while drowning
you reach for his hand
you live in denial

you want to be saved
by someone who makes love
an unsafe place

she wore every face but her own

each scar is a confession of strength and survival

her heart is too pure
for the places it's been

---

for once, she wanted
to be surprised
and not disappointed

but people are
who they've always been
pieces of shit
pretending to be gold

---

he left, and he should stay gone

he left

and so should you

---

she's always thinking
about the feelings she hides
her pain hidden behind
a million "i'm okays"
still pretending to be fine

---

this world
would feel incomplete
without you

keep fighting
keep surviving
keep living
please stay

"I miss you," she whispered while staring at her reflection. Looking for the woman she lost while loving someone incapable of caring for her heart.

---

you're extraordinary

stay away from mediocre men

who only wish to waste your time

It's hard not to be loud about the things you genuinely love. Understand this when he decides to be silent about you.

Your life is a montage of survival and strength.
A story worth being celebrated.

It may not feel like it. But you are becoming a stronger version of who you've been. I know it gets difficult, believing in this idea that you are more than your brokenness.

---

your heart is broken
but true love will work
its way through the cracks

---

stop acting like you're weak

you are the definition of a powerful woman

on the verge of letting go and moving on

---

be with someone who moves you

like the moon drifts through the night sky

---

you lose her trust

you lose your future

---

the sound of rolling thunder
rumbling its way through her heart
while a thousand fires burn
within her soul

wild, ember.

you are a wild ember glow
sparking the midnight sky
you roll like thunder
with flashes of lightning
inside your broken heart

you are a beautiful storm of fire
raging toward peace
running toward love
chasing what you deserve

July 22, 2019.

How could your birthday not matter to him? Last year, he gave you nothing, and this year, he forgot about you altogether. I guess I shouldn't be surprised. Your life is filled with bumps and bruises that he caused, due to not being there to catch you whenever you'd fall. I watch our son every day and wonder to myself, how could a father and mother do so little for their kids? How could a father leave his daughter vulnerable out in the pasture with the wolves? And how could your mother go absent, not there to teach you how to have a presence? Luckily, you were able to teach yourself how to cultivate and maintain your magic. Luckily, you were strong when they were weak, and I'm proud of you for being all that you could be, even when they set you up to fail.

beyond the fourth wall.

You're stuck between wanting to feel everything and the desire to be numb. You want to be alone, but you're afraid of the loneliness that might arrive while you're on your own. You say you want something real, but time and time again, you've chosen to stay with someone who has proven to be fraudulent in more ways than one. It hurts, but you survive. You're in pain, and yet you smile. You realize that moving on is your best bet, but you've yet to access the courage to leave. For some odd reason, you feel guilty for wanting to let go. All in a while, the person you're with doesn't feel guilty whenever they hurt you. For so long, you've put others first while allowing yourself to be secondary or never chosen at all, and I think that it's past due that you decide to choose yourself. I know you love this person, but what's love in a relationship with someone who treats you like they hate you, and what's effort in a relationship with someone who is never truly willing to try for you? There shouldn't be an obligation to stay, but you feel it. You feel it every time you're ready to walk out of that door. It's torture. Waiting around for something that may not happen, thinking they'll change when they never will—dreaming of a future with someone who feels more like a dead end. Someone who will never be the person they promised to be.

Who would you become if you left them right now? What would you do with the opportunity to pour more of your love into yourself? How would it feel to finally be in a position to receive real love from someone capable of appreciating all that you give? I need you to start asking yourself real questions like this. I need you to want more for yourself, because this relationship you've settled for is stale, confusing, and lacking whatever substance you'd need to feel loved. I'm not judging you. I completely understand why you've stayed for so long. You're strong enough to love unconditionally, you're devoted, and you're not one to quit, but isn't it hell, staying with the one who has abandoned you several times? Aren't you tired of being hurt when you should be loved for who you are and everything you have in your heart to share? You don't have to answer this right now, but all I ask is that when you put down this book that you begin to think about everything that occupies your time and begin to cut away the things that no longer fit into your present. You can't find love until you love yourself, and most times, the love of self will keep you on the path to a healthy relationship.

Fri 8:09pm.

I don't know when you'll read this or where you'll be when you find these words. Hopefully somewhere safe with someone who makes you happy, doing something that brings you peace. But if none of this is true for you, and you are to find these words amid heartbreak, I hope you know that you are fully deserving of a love that helps you grow. I hope you find a love that makes you forget about how painful it felt to love the wrong person.

---

gracefully
she walked through
the storm

she never bowed
to the rain

---

it will be hard to leave
until it gets harder to stay

Because women don't always know that men often send those same texts to several women at a time, it's almost as if they go fishing with lies as their bait, hoping to get a bite. He wants you to feel special, and maybe you do. Maybe that text expressed everything you've been wanting to hear. Maybe that message arrived at the right moment, but it's designed to be and feel that way. How many times have you received an "I miss you" text from someone who ended up hurting you once more?

I think it's interesting that after you get your heart broken, your friends suggest that you go out and surround yourself with the same type of people who will hurt your heart. You go out to a club that is filled with individuals who mirror the same characteristics as your ex, while attempting to have fun in a room that is occupied by people who may be harmful for your soul. You want to feel better, and despite that temporary high you get while pretending that everything is okay, you've put yourself in an environment that will almost certainly cause you to repeat the same mistakes and possibly force you into another situation that resembles the relationship you were trying to move on from. Just a thought, something to think about.

You can't keep giving your attention, time, energy, and love to a person who isn't willing to work for those things. Trying harder for someone who isn't willing to give you the least bit of their energy will just make you feel stuck.

Truth is . . . you're going to go through hardship before it gets any easier. You're going to go through pain before you can reach bliss. Don't give up on the peace and love you know you deserve. Please keep going.

in position.

Heavy manipulation, the way he makes you feel bad for demanding what you deserve. You're not clingy for wanting to be loved. You're not nagging when trying to hold him accountable for his actions. You're not asking for too much when you insist that he makes the same amount of effort as you've made. You don't have to feel guilty for wanting to be chosen. You don't have to feel bad for wanting to leave behind someone who isn't willing to do much to make you stay. Don't allow him the power to make you feel like you're overreacting when all you're asking for is respect and love. There's nothing wrong with wanting to feel like you matter in your relationship.

I hate that you've allowed them to silence you. You walk on eggshells just to appease someone who has never actually considered how you may feel in this particular relationship. And you continue to settle because you're afraid of losing a person who doesn't even deserve to keep you. And the longer you hold on to that person, the more you lose yourself. I'm not judging you for staying, I get it. You don't want to give up on someone you love, but energy invested into a toxic relationship is energy wasted. You have two choices in the end: Hold on to the one person who will destroy any hopes of you knowing what true love feels like, or choose yourself and pour all that you have into your own peace of mind. Choose yourself because, right now, you are deserving of the love you've wasted on others. Choose yourself and you'll be in position for something beautiful to finally happen.

stop providing your light

to people who push you toward darkness

But isn't that the problem? You put others first and end up coming in last because you do more for others than they'll ever do for you, and as much as you think that this makes you a good person, it doesn't. How can you be a good person when you're so unkind to yourself? How can you be so good to others and yet so neglectful to yourself at the same time? The only reward in helping those who will never help you is a life that is filled with regret and loneliness. One day you'll look back and wish you lived instead of living a life of doing for others.

Your father half-asses everything, but you accept it. Maybe this is why you've settled for mediocre relationships with men who are only capable of giving a half-ass love, if any at all.

The same man who was supposed to protect you left you with no shield, no sword, and so you were tasked to fight off the wolves with your bare hands. There's no shame in admitting that you lost a few of those battles, but the irony of it all is that your father left you vulnerable to men who were just as weak as he is.

Life is beautiful when you begin to say no to all the people who were never worthy of a yes.

Stop searching for closure from a man who wasn't even capable of comprehending your worth and love.

Love me as if there is no one else you'll ever need or want

Your relationship is shelter, your partner is a home. Some are beautiful cabins, homes that could house a family, lofts, skyrises, or mansions, while others are run-down places with faulty wiring and roofs that leak whenever it rains. What type of relationship are you in? What type of home is your partner?

---

your soul is unsettled
your eyes wander recklessly
through the darkness
in search of light
your heart is aching
but no-one knows why

you are beautiful
an all-powerful being
with magic rushing
through your veins

in the silence.

i hear her
silently sitting there
wearing a smile
that dreadful mask
hiding her truth behind soft lips
and bright eyes
that appear to be sad

i hear her
saying nothing
silent screams
blister the air like winter
she sits still like cold air
frozen in sadness
pretending to be happy

i hear her
because i care
i hear her
i wish to listen

You

It's after 10 in the evening, and you've been glancing at your phone every three minutes, awaiting a notification or vibration as an indication that he has finally responded to that text message you sent hours ago. You've become so anxious waiting patiently for him to reach out to you. You're always texting first, you're always the one to reach out. You're always the one in waiting, as it would seem that he prefers to take his time and reply whenever it's convenient for him.

Eleven rolls around, and you're still sitting there. You begin to create a text, then after a brief moment of thought, you decide to delete the text. You don't want to seem clingy, needy, or overeager, but let's be honest: you wonder what the fuck he could be doing that is keeping him so busy that he's not able to respond. It's noon, and you receive a text from him. It's short, one-worded, non-enthusiastic, as always, and once your phone vibrates to show that you have one incoming text, you're excited a little, but you're also upset. Feelings of neglect have already taken their toll on you, and you're merely uncertain, angry, curious, but still a bit glad that he decided to reach out.

Him

He saw your text. He looked at your text earlier that day and decided not to respond. His friends are always bragging about the woman they keep waiting. They live by this code of making a woman wonder, forcing her to feel confused. They never really want women to know how much or how little they like them. It's part of a game, a game they've learned to play well. Give her enough to cause her to catch feelings, give her just enough of your time, then pull away, leaving her to pine and sit anxiously awaiting a response. He looked at your text, then decided at that moment how many hours he'd let pass before responding.

He waited because he knows you'll wait around for him, no matter what, or at least that's what he thinks. See, you're just not that important, you're not a priority in his life. And to top it all off, he texted you at that hour, the exact hour in which you'd given up hope that you'd get a response, because his girlfriend is finally asleep. Once she's asleep, he's free. He's free to waste your time.

Morning arrives, and the cycle continues because you don't know. But now you do, and now it all makes sense. You are being sent to voice mail when you call. He's always unreachable, he's rarely consistent, and he never seems to get "that text message" or somehow doesn't have a chance to text you at a reasonable hour. There's no time for you because his time is invested elsewhere, but at least you know now. At least you have the answer to your questions. Stop entertaining those who refuse to make an effort as far as you're concerned.

After you've been hurt, everything then becomes "too good to be true." You meet someone who makes you happy, and yet you act as if you're afraid of this newfound joy because of a situation within your past when that joy turned out to be nothing, but you can't allow your past to keep you from moving forward and into a better future with someone new.

The only way to discover if it's real is to let go of that nagging thought that "this is too good to be true." Stop cheating yourself because of your past and start treating yourself to a brighter future. Take chances, and love will find its way to you.

---

you're beautiful

something you refuse to believe

you're good enough

something they fail to tell you

you deserve better

sounds cliché, but it's true

i've observed so many strong, real, intelligent,
and loyal women

put up with behaviors that are beneath them

your smile becomes a mask, your laughter
neglected . . .

your happiness on life support, nearly dying
because you've settled

for less than you deserve

Please don't let him make you feel guilty for wanting to be cherished and loved.

---

i know you wish to hold on
you're afraid of letting go
you're hoping for change
but change will not arrive

do not water dead flowers
do not stay where you aren't loved

---

too often you distract yourself
with a new relationship
you smile to keep from crying
you do so much pretending
but you are not healed

---

honest enough to say i miss you

strong enough not to take you back

---

of course, he'll live without you
but he'll eventually die one day
without knowing the magnitude
of the love you were trying to give him
before he betrayed your trust

---

he broke her heart
then complained
that she was heartless

---

i don't think she's cold

i just think she's smart enough

not to waste her warmth on you

---

give me a love

that never grows tired

give me a love

that isn't compromised by time

---

she built her own wings
she mastered the art of flight
and she flew above and over
anyone who wished to keep her grounded

---

she wasn't sad anymore

yes, it was dark, but she made her own light

and found her way back to herself again

---

that was her magic

the way she loved

like she'd never been hurt

---

and sometimes she hides

because she knows that the one

who truly loves her

will see everything she's locked away

---

it's hard, you know
training your lips to smile
while your heart is falling apart

---

they chase stars
but you are the moon
bigger, brighter
and nothing in the night sky
compares to you

---

you are worth
the attention
and devotion
they're not giving you

---

saying no to him
meant saying yes
to yourself

---

something about her
feels like a prayer
she embodies all the things
that i would hope for

---

she felt like breaking

but fought instead

---

you are a universe
of possibilities,
and it's a shame
he couldn't see it

---

your pain is your candle
you learn your strength
by getting hurt

Don't get me wrong, the stars are beautiful; but you, my dear, are more than that. You have always been the moon in a pale-gray sky. Even in darkness, you had more to love, more to see. So much more to appreciate.

---

no one is you
nothing and no one
can compete

---

burn some bridges
for light in the darkness
and for warmth in the winter

It's about time you started getting the type of love and dedication you've wasted on others.

---

happy to be alone
is the woman
who has loved and been hurt
happy to be alone
is the woman
who would rather wait
for something real
than settle for something
that feels like nothing

---

wanting him to be the one
is not enough to make him
worthy of you

---

don't you need rest
after piecing every bit
of your heart back together

it's okay to take a permanent break
from choosing those
who won't choose you

---

there were times
in which she felt alone
there were times
when all she wanted
was to fill that void
within her heart
there were times
when she just wanted
to share the things kept
sacred within her soul
there was a time
when she realized
that being alone
meant being available
to the one deserving
of her company
and this time
she's choosing herself
this time she's decided
that the path to true love
exists within

---

the night sky was her canvas
and she was the moon
supplying her own light
as she sat there alone

she was a Queen
without a King
she was royal
but by herself
still deserving
of the throne
and she refused
to settle for less

We judge women based on the ratio of ass, hips, and waist. We've literally turned them into numbers that are far less than their value. We objectify them so much that we're incapable of realizing what we have when in the presence of a good woman. Too lazy to dig deeper to find something within them that is truly rare and significant, we hop from woman to woman, searching, receiving what we think we want yet never truly satisfied.

And that's why we stay longer than we should, because it hurts to watch something you love transform into something you should hate, something that hurts your heart and soul. We sit and wait for it to return to its original state. We go through the pain of investing our hope into a hopeless situation, in denial as we ignore the fact that what we see was always there and what is now will always be. And so the heart begins to break. It shatters because you're not ready to move on, but you know you must move forward without the person you thought you needed.

Love is having someone beside you to confront your demons. Someone willing and ready to stand beneath stormy clouds with you and not be moved. Someone patient with your sadness while assuring you that things will get better. Love is out there, love lives within, and the romantic love you wish for will arrive. Never give up on your idea of what being in love means.

I'm just not who I was before you. I allowed you into a place untouched by the hands of anyone. I held the door open just so that you could walk in and make a home out of me. You took my willingness, my acceptance and destroyed the insides of my heart. You took the trust that I gave unto you and threw it away as if to say, "This is garbage." Before you, I was different. After you, I'll never be the same.

I'd rather you fall in love with the parts of me that no one cares to know. Only then would you truly understand what it means to love me.

---

and that's your problem
you're too good at holding on
too strong to let go
too loyal to walk away
too kind to leave
even after he's abandoned you
you're too good at giving yourself
to someone too stupid
to see the true worth
in all that you do
and i hope you find the strength
to eventually choose yourself
it's time to be kinder
to your own heart

I think she knew she'd have to let go, yet she held on to parts of him that no longer existed. There were times when she'd look into his eyes and see nothing, times when he'd say, "I'm sorry," and she'd force herself to believe it. The arguing disguised as passion. The fighting disguised as love. How is it that the man who once pledged his allegiance to your heart is now the one forcing you to pick up the pieces by yourself after he broke it? And why are you so willing to take him back even after he's proven time and time again that he's not worth the love you've given him?

---

we could have been great
but you insisted on being mediocre
you placed limits on us
and what we could be
so i chose myself
i deserved more
i chose me
instead of us
and that's when
the healing began

anger based.

What upsets me is that you smile in their faces while they laugh and joke about you behind your back. You make every effort to make them feel special, all while they overlook you as often as they can. They're supposed to be the ones to protect you from the coldness of this world, and yet they bring about winter in your heart. And even though you feel broken, you still love them with whatever you have left. That's what bothers me the most. Witnessing you give everything to a group of people who do nothing but disappoint you. And your only reason for allowing them to hurt you is because they're family.

self, safe.

Aren't you tired of feeling confused, abused verbally by the same mouth that claimed to love you? Only to leave your heart aching after every argument you enter? You left the last time feeling like less than you were before—your self-esteem buried beneath a rubble of uncertainty. You want things to get better, you hope for change. You rearrange everything about yourself to appease a person who isn't concerned about your peace of mind. You find time to give while they refuse to make time for you. You are always fighting, not realizing that using that energy on someone like this will still amount to a losing battle. You ignore your scars because they remind you that you should move on. You see the stains on the wall, and you decide to paint over them. You know the truth and what you must do, but you move blindly into love with no regard for your own heart. I wish you knew of your own strength. I wish you'd realize that it's time to keep yourself safe.

---

she's committed to herself

she's devoted to finding the love

that lives within

---

i wish your father tried harder
i wish more effort was placed into you
i wish he was more present
more loving, more protective
of your heart

i wish your mother tried harder
i wish more effort was invested into you
i wish she was more present
more loving, more protective
of your heart

the war and your survival.

How do you do it? How do you make it through the type of nights that would drown others? How do you survive the waves of unhappiness? Sadness comes knocking at your door, and the more you ignore it, the louder it gets as midnight creeps toward your window, pushing the moon higher than before. You're unreal, but you're here, fighting amid the night sky and dreaming beneath the light of the moon. You're unreal, but you're here, a traveler in search of love and understanding. You didn't set out to get hurt, but it happened. But you continue to move forward, and you refuse to give up. There are nights when the darkness becomes overwhelming; the later it gets, the more your heart seems to sink into itself—such a terrible feeling, one that is hard to explain. You scream into your pillow, your eyes tightly shut. You are hoping that when you open them and reemerge from the rivers of pain that everything will be made different and you'll be able to breathe freely again, even if it isn't. If all remains the same and the heartache arrives at the same time every night, you'll still do it, and you'll still be here surviving. You'll still be here, fighting yet another war. And I'll again wonder how you do what you've always done.

hourglass.

When you think about it, there's so little time to retrieve the love you say you want. So little time that there's not much room for error, and yet here you are. Feeling around in the dark for a love that isn't even there. We always meet this way, don't we? Your heart is broken, and so you stumble upon my words intentionally. Looking for yet another reminder as to why you should leave the person you're with. It's been years now, and your heart has felt this uneasiness for far too long—longer than you deserve. I'll tell you to move on, and you'll respond and say it's easier said than done, and that saying will force you into a cycle in which you decide to hold on to one person who is no longer deserving of your love. Moving on is easier said than done, but it has never been impossible. This world is made up of people who have decided that they deserve more, and the only way to bring them closer to a love that matters is to leave behind the person who has made them feel like they don't matter.

Maybe these words will reach the person who is tired of fighting for someone who does nothing but destroy their happiness. Perhaps these words will reach the individual who has reached their breaking point and is ready to break free. Maybe these words will reach someone like you, a person who knows that they deserve so much more but has felt stuck in their relationship because of time invested and love given. You're reading this now for a reason, you picked up this book for a reason, and I know that you won't be able to leave overnight. I'm aware that it takes time, but don't waste the time you have left searching for real love in a fraudulent person. Don't waste whatever time you have left trying to love someone who has proven to be incapable of being strong enough to care for you in the way you need.

---

move on

fuck him

be brave

Correct me if I'm wrong, but I think it hurts because you genuinely give a fuck. It hurts because even though you want to hold on, you know that letting go is the best thing you could do for your future, and that doesn't make it any easier.

---

when you begin

to search for real love

seek yourself

---

she grew silent
like a flower in winter
he was no longer
worthy of her words
and so she said nothing
on her way out

---

the saddest eyes i've ever seen
belonged to a woman
surrounded by friends
in a nightclub

---

be empty

then fill your heart

with more of yourself

---

ignore what he said

observe what he does

---

remarkable

the way she collapses

yet catches herself

---

forever is fractured by lies and betrayal

---

he's been your nightmare

wake up

someone you need
is searching for you

---

she understands the rain

because she too is used to falling

---

i am a victim of hoping
for something that can't happen

---

you are worthy of your love

you are worthy of your forgiveness

you are worthy of your kindness

start choosing yourself

her soul

a rainbow

of infinite vibrance

---

she made herself at home

within her own arms

---

you are allowed
to burn bridges
that no longer
deserve to reach you

---

feel what you need to feel
say what lives within your heart
and never hold on to things
that don't belong in your life

---

he can't love you

like you love you

move closer to yourself

---

she dreams of being loved

the way she loves

I'll say this. Never listen to anyone who tells you that real love doesn't exist. There are two versions of a broken heart. One where a person stops believing in love and one where a person continues forward in search of something real, no matter how hurt they may feel. I'm glad that my wife continued after heartbreak. I'm glad my wife never gave up on the idea of finding real love. If my wife believed that real love didn't exist, then we wouldn't have found each other. I'm looking at my son right now, and he's a representation of what happens when real love wins. It's so easy to give up on love after you've been betrayed many times, but for the ones who haven't lost hope . . . I can assure you that no matter how broken you may feel, there is someone in the world searching for someone like you. I had always been searching for my wife, and this is why I know love is real, and I don't believe that I'm the only man on this earth who is capable of loving one woman and reciprocating the love she gives me. Don't give up. Don't let heartbreak dictate your future and your beliefs. Don't give your ex that power.

8/22/19.

You're reaching for someone who is the cause of your pain—reaching for someone who is the reason that you're sinking, nearly drowning. You put so much hope into a person who has often left you hopeless. Do you not remember why your heart is breaking? Do you not remember why your soul is weary? Aren't you tired of pretending to be happy when you're not, pretending that this is love when it feels like hate?

I'm tired of always being present in your absence. I'm tired of trying harder when you make no effort. I'm tired of giving a love that is never reciprocated—tired of forgiving you when you're not genuinely sorry. I'm tired of giving second chances when you never deserved the first. I'm tired of pretending that everything is fine while I continue to fall apart inside. I'm tired of being in love alone. I'm just tired.

I thank you when you've done nothing to help. I praise you for all the things I wish you'd do. I celebrate you even as you ignore my accomplishments. I paint you with vibrance, but you've always been a dull color, gray. I say to myself, "Maybe it'll get better, I have to stay longer to see it through," when honestly I should look into your eyes and whisper, "Fuck you."

There are moments when I wish I had a time machine. I'd use it to go back to the moment we met and avoid you at all costs. Because being here with you has been a waste of my future.

The only future you have by holding on to the wrong person is a life that will never know what it means to be loved truly.

---

you are a needed phenomenon
like rain falling in the middle of the desert
and if he can't realize that your existence
can be summed up as a rare occurrence
then he doesn't deserve you

Tell me why you're crying, tell me why you decide to stay where you're not appreciated. Don't you remember what it felt like to be happy on your own, free from heartache? Free from him and his bullshit? Tell me why you've decided to settle, struggling to survive the impact of his disrespect and disregard for your emotional well-being. Are you crying because you wish to hold on longer, or is it that you're ready to let go but you're afraid?

You will find everything you've ever needed in the absence of everyone who couldn't appreciate you.

Sometimes people can't comprehend the power of your love until it's taken away from them without an explanation.

I think you ought to be in love with yourself a little deeper.

---

sadness leaves

but it never dies

---

it's been a long time

since you've chosen yourself

---

the moon
is most visible
during darkness
and so is your strength

---

whatever causes the rain
in your soul and the pain
in your heart
leave it behind

---

sometimes you get better

sometimes you're just different

---

when you dream of true love

i hope you dream of yourself

---

you want so many things

and you want it from

the wrong person

her tears are full of ghosts
remnants of heartbreak

---

she's been through hell
but there's still heaven
in her bones

---

midnight was nothing more than

a cemetery for dead stars

---

if he loved you

he'd choose the peace

in your heart

instead of chaos and confusion

---

you love him

you're just not willing

to allow yourself to stay any longer

because you refuse to let him hurt you

He knew he wasn't shit when he approached you. He knowingly wasted your time. He knew damn well that he was incapable of fully comprehending your worth, and even though that shit hurt you, even though your heart has been aching, soul weary, restless, unable to sleep, I hope you still remember what you're worth, and I hope you take all the energy and love and time that you've invested in him and give it entirely to yourself. I hope this reaches you, the one who needs this the most.

---

it almost feels as if
your puzzle piece isn't meant
to fit anyone
but you keep going
you keep loving
and that's brave

Go someplace where you feel free. Far away from him and his bullshit. Someplace where your soul can finally be at ease.

Love isn't supposed to feel terrible. Love is supposed to destroy the most terrible things.

You're almost there, just a little bit longer now. Keep your head up, guard your heart, and love yourself through this storm.

Sometimes I don't want to be human. Aching for something that I can never find, empty from giving my all without any of it being reciprocated. Falling in love alone then forced to pick up the pieces of my own heart. Who wants to be human when it hurts this much?

Something good happening with someone good enough to love me in the way I need.

---

never mind the summer

if you wish to find winter

look into my soul

---

and i once thought
feeling nothing was safer
until being numb
kept me from finding you

scene fifty-two.

This life, your life. You've done so much of it alone. You've carried yourself through flames, you've reached for your own hand successfully while drowning. You're remarkable even when you won't believe it. No cape, just strength. The power to hold yourself up whenever you fear falling. Instead of looking to others, you save yourself. You are the hero you've always needed. You are the hero you deserve.

your reality.

I was watching this reality show with my wife the other night. It's a show that profiles the lives of strangers getting married, and the viewer gets the opportunity to witness two people attempt to cultivate and maintain a marriage. There was an episode in which the guy, newly married to his wife, began to stay out at all hours of the night, sometimes returning days later. We watched the wife nearly torment herself while pacing back and forth in their apartment and sending texts that were ignored. Phone calls sent to voice mail, a heart aching because it felt neglected. All of this happened, and when he finally returned home, though she was upset, she found a way to excuse his behavior just enough to feel the need to reward him.

This got me to thinking about you, the person reading this now. How many times have you made excuses for someone who hurt you? How many times have you ignored the screaming truth, just so that you could feel justified in giving that person another opportunity to disappoint you? I think the world and its teachings have been so unkind to the mind of women, instructing them to do more when the people in their lives do nothing—teaching them to feel bad about demanding what they deserve, being made to feel like you're asking for too much when it comes to being loved and feeling loved. It hurts me to think that someone can mistreat you, break your heart, and you could still love them with every piece of you scattered across the floor.

I'm not judging you. I want the best for you. I want you to know what it means to be fully appreciated. Life is too short to be in a relationship that feels like hell. A relationship that drains and destroys you. Why are you so hard on yourself and so easy on someone who never makes it easy for you?

definitively you.

Define your value, take power away from others who wish to treat you as if you're not good enough. Understand your worth and demand that you be treated with respect and love. Be ready to walk away from the people who prove to be unworthy of standing beside you. Stop giving second chances to individuals who did nothing but disappoint you from the first, and start choosing yourself. Especially while feeling overlooked by those you care about the most. Understand that you are not obligated to stay in any relationship that isn't encouraging you to grow. Understand that you do not have to feel bad about wanting what you give; there's nothing wrong with demanding what you believe you deserve. It's time to take control of your future by placing certain people in your past.

I wonder if your shadow grows weary of you dragging it into relationships that were never worthy of your presence.

It's like the longer you hold on to the wrong person, the further you are from the type of relationship you feel you deserve.

Heartbreak will alter the way you feel about relationships, but don't let the pain keep you from discovering the right person to love.

You fear being alone, and so you've chosen to be with the one who makes you feel the most lonely. You want to be loved, but you've decided to hold on to one who seems to hate the idea of you being happy.

Choosing yourself means deciding to be happy, despite your feelings for the wrong person.

Choosing yourself means giving yourself a second chance at peace.

---

some will fall

you will stand

---

the pain you feel now

is not your forever

You've had this terrible feeling living inside your bones, and it's time to listen to what the aches are trying to tell you.

For you, beauty is much more than the surface. Beautiful is the way you fight for what you deserve. Beautiful is how you survive feeling broken.

She was tired emotionally, but she had just enough left to move on with her life.

---

she sounds like music

the sound of a song

that symbolizes a devotion to herself

---

one day you'll make sense

to the only one strong enough

to hear the pain behind your silence

Give up the person who forced you to give up your smile.

Maybe the one you're supposed to be with is distracted by the wrong person also.

Be kinder to the woman crying back at you in the mirror.

scene fifty-three.

I honestly wish I could do more for you, and I wish there were magic words that I could spell out that would assist you in breaking free from the bondage of being with someone whose only intention is to use and abuse you. I've read back over so much of the content in this book, and I genuinely hope that my intentions were not lost and that maybe you found something that could motivate you to move forward with your life. But still, I wish there were more that I could do for you. To the heart that is breaking, the soul that is weary, and the mind that is currently struggling with the idea of detaching from the person you believed would reciprocate the love you've given to them: maybe you're reading this in search of an answer. An answer that I'm not sure that I have. But whoever you are and whenever you get the chance to read this, I hope you find the magic in letting go. I hope you discover the reward for moving on.

I want you to know that, despite the heartache that has always filled your heart, and even though you're used to being hurt, you still deserve a love that doesn't cause you anguish. You still deserve a love that is everlasting and true. I get it, you've been with the wrong person for so long that you've nearly given up on this idea of true love. You've decided to stay because of the time and energy you've invested, but imagine if you gave that same time and energy to someone capable of reciprocating the things you throw their way. Imagine how peaceful it would be to find someone who considers you always.

It just happens. You don't plan for it, but when it happens, you embrace the idea with an open mind. It's so good in the beginning, that feeling of perfection. Ignorance is bliss, and that feeling of bliss can cause you to be blind to the reality of what may be happening. Time becomes your energy because the more you invest, the closer you are to figuring out that the love you believed to be real may have just been a manipulative lie. Empty promises made in an effort to make you vulnerable enough to share the energy they never deserved. It just happens that way, and it happens to the best of you—the best of us.

You've been running from yourself lately, afraid of what will happen when you finally catch up. Change can be a scary thing, but you must never pass up the opportunity to grow. You're evolving into everything they said you'd never be, and that's beautiful. That is a change worth embracing.

Despite the change in the weather, despite the storm, she went on growing, blooming, and becoming more of everything she was meant to be.

I can't fault you for wanting to walk away from people who fail to respect you, and no, I don't think you should feel bad for distancing yourself from them.

broken girls
keep poems
inside their hearts
that should be celebrated
and revered

---

you can reach for others
you can hope that they save you
or you can reach for yourself
because in the midst
of needing to be saved
the only arms long enough to reach you
the only hands strong enough
to protect you are yours

---

be your own companion
while you wait to be loved
by someone other than yourself

Stop holding on to what you should have left behind.

You never belonged to him. Don't let him own your emotions.

---

pain seals itself in our tears
cry because that's the way
toward the freedom to feel joy

You're trying to fit real feelings into a fraudulent relationship. Stop.

---

the moon knows her name

midnight keeps calling

answer below.

How much of night do you waste on thinking about what you could have done better in a relationship with someone who refuses to even try? How much of midnight have you used to hide your tears behind a shade of black? How much are you willing to lose in a relationship that drains you so much that you don't even have the energy to sleep? How long will you stay with someone who will never grow?

Remind yourself that you deserve better by letting go of the person who doesn't deserve you.

You're built for this. The part where fear creeps up into your mind whenever you think about leaving or the pain that arrives when trying to survive the breakup. You're built for the heartache, and you have the strength to get through it. The courage to move on lives within you, use it.

How is it that you feel bad about leaving him,
but he never gives a fuck about hurting you?

Purge the idea of him from your heart by accepting the fact that he's always been too weak to appreciate your presence.

You had greatness in you all along. You just had to find your fire.

Find your fire and burn through everything that no longer fits into your life.

You will wake up from this nightmare. You will dream dreams worth dreaming when you detach from the things and the people who hurt you.

Don't let a day go by without reminding yourself that you are worthy of a love that makes you feel safe.

What happens to your dreams when you can't sleep.

Dear woman,

You're holding this book, reading these words. I'm not sure where you are or what time it will be at the moment you read this, but I know your heart is heavy with pain and your mind is filled with confusion. You've been holding on to someone who was never worth it, loving someone incapable of loving you back. You stay because you've invested too much into this relationship to leave, but as you read this, you realize that, more than ever, it's time to let go. I admire your patience, but life is too short to wait around for someone to be something they can't. I admire your strength, but instead of using all you have to hold on, you have to use that same strength to move on with your life. We're strangers at this moment, and though we may not know one another, I happen to know what currently lives within your heart. I wish you knew that there was magic living beneath your bones. I wish you knew that you have always been more than enough. I wish you knew that you are strong enough to set yourself free. Maybe this isn't enough, and perhaps you'll miss this message. No matter what happens, I can't give up on you, and I hope you don't give up on yourself. These words were written for the woman who is strong but tired. The woman who sometimes forgets to choose herself. These words are for the woman who, despite feeling broken, decides to survive. It's time to walk away, be brave.

Sincerely, a stranger who cares,

r.h. Sin

---

you wear sadness as a winter coat
draped over your body so perfectly
hanging on to your shoulders for dear life
as it blows in the wind

---

they were never lovers
they never loved me
i tried to use them for warmth
but in the end, i shivered alone
in the cold of the night

And you were broken just as much I was. Our scars similar, our wounds the same. Those sad eyes were looking back at me as if I had the answers, and even though I wish I had, I was struggling just as much as you were. I was bored with the overdone physical show of tainted affection and the emptiness that occurred after the act was over. We were searching for more, and more brought us to each other. I still think about that, and I spend sleepless nights lying next to you, dreaming while awake of the moment our brokenness pushed us into each other's arms, and that's why, deep down, I'm grateful for the pain. It all began not because I was looking for a good fuck. I just wanted someone to live a good life with.

---

you're afraid
that you're going to be
the only one who remembers
everything you wish to forget

---

old friends

new strangers

that's what we've become

be careful who you build

your dreams on

I know it's hard because you've been hurt so many fucking times, but you are worth finding. You are worth loving.

---

the way you survive is art

you're becoming a masterpiece

---

peace dwells within you
and despite the chaos in this world
there is a calm wherever you go
there is bliss in your presence

Perhaps he was never what you needed, and you only believed in him because he was capable of telling you everything you wanted to hear whenever you needed to hear it.

Self-love is the best practice of affection.

I wish you could remember
entered your life. I know you
he was someone worth letting in,
whatever it is you need to help you hold
obsess over the good times, blurring out the
bad. Ignoring the warning signs and red flags,
but deep down, you know what you must do.
Deep down, you're unhappy, and behind that
smile is everything you've kept to yourself. And
I wish you'd remember how happier you were
before he decided to destroy your peace. I wish
you could remember how to find the courage
that has already lived within your heart, and
more than anything, and I wish you knew that
you'd be fine without him in your life. I know
you've invested so much of yourself into him
and the relationship, but you must understand
that nothing will make a difference in a
relationship with someone who would rather
hurt you than love you. None of that will ever
make a difference to someone who has always
been too weak to stand beside you. I know
you've dedicated your life to him, and for that, I
dedicate these words to you. There is a goddess-
like power that resides deep within everything
that you are, and it is waiting to be used on your
path to emotional freedom. It's time to break
away from the man who will never deserve you.

I think you need to know that it is entirely okay to detach from members of your family who cause nothing but pain and discomfort in your life. I think it's okay for you to break up with family members who are toxic and disappointing. "Family" is not a word that should cause you to compromise.

You've been dancing around the truth for so long that you've learned to move willingly with the lies he tells you. And I wish you'd stop allowing him to return when he never meant to stay in the first place.

---

while other poets wish
to only show off their ability
to use words you'll never understand
or to reference ideas too complex
for even themselves

i choose to speak to you
and your heart

while the other writers
are prisoners of their vanity
and pursuit of fame

i'm running after you
trying to prevent you
from throwing your life away
for a lover who will never love you

Maybe you don't give a fuck about what I have to say. Perhaps I'm too much of a stranger to matter to you, but that won't make me give up on this idea of you finally being happy on your own and in your relationship. I know moving on is easier said than done, but you are capable of walking away from anyone who refuses to choose you. Your heart has seen a fair share of heartache, but you always find a way to survive, and every time your heart breaks, you rise stronger than before. You're worth everything you've been wanting. You deserve a love that will help and encourage you to grow. It's time to choose yourself. It's time to break free. You are more than enough, and you are fully capable of freeing yourself. I refuse to give up on you. Please, don't give up on yourself.

---

she is a museum of wild art
strokes of strength
and courage on a canvas

Make a list of what you want, need, and deserve. Then remove people from your life who are keeping you from everything on that list.

Consider that this life we lead is entirely too short, made shorter by the time we spend on people who were never worth our energy. You've already lost so much of your time as is, what sense would it make to give him more of you when he's never willing to appreciate all that it is you have to offer?

Blood may be thicker than water, but it will never be more important than peace of mind and joy within the heart.

A family is just a group of titles until the individuals in your family give more meaning to their roles by showing up when the time comes.

strangely familiar.

Sometimes I think of you, but not in the way that others do. See, we're strangers, and what that means is that I don't actually know your name and maybe I don't know what you look like, but that doesn't mean I can't deem you familiar. You seem like someone so sad that you smile often. You're one of those women who search for love in all the places it'll never exist. And no matter how large a heart you have and no matter how much you give, none of it seems to work, and because of this, you feel like a failure. You feel like giving up on this idea of true love because every relationship you've entered has turned your heart a bit colder. And so, sometimes I think of you. The thought of you and what you're going through runs through my mind like a tornado. This storm, though powerful, is not one I run from but one I willingly chase until I feel as lost as you.

Don't you feel lost? Doesn't it feel like everything you've wanted doesn't exist? Do you feel like you're running toward a dead end, or maybe you feel like there's no end in sight for the heartache you feel? The nights drain you, the nighttime sky a symbol for what you think—struggling to find light beneath a half-moon. You fight wars that no one will know about. Your heart screams things no one will ever hear, or at least you thought so. I want so badly for you to read this. I need you to know that you are not alone, and even in a crowded night, full of hearts breaking just like yours, I feel you, and sometimes I think of you.

All of everything you've ever given was always more than enough. You were giving it to someone incapable of comprehending all that you've ever been.

The heart is more honest at midnight when it is too tired to lie to itself.

Uncertainty has no place in a relationship. The confusion drains the heart of its energy to love.

He was never a loss. You learn this when you realize that his absence just gave you more time to love yourself.

The sad truth is that lonely people tend to choose others who will lead them to more loneliness.

The love you imagined is real, just not with him.

---

you are rain
when the roots
need it most
you are light
in the silence
of midnight

---

you feel sadness

but you are still worthy

you feel broken

but you are still powerful

---

she still loves him

but she's no longer willing

to compromise her heart

---

if you wait for him,
you'll be furthest
from joy

if you hold on to him,
your heart will know nothing
but heartache and disappointment

his ghost lives in her tears

---

do not lose who you've been
to keep a man who will never
appreciate all that you are

---

the more you drown
the thought of him
the closer you drift
toward peace

---

in silence

we say a form of nothing

that means so much

Right now, you wonder if you should stay,.and that alone is a sign.

---

some silence
is harsher
than screaming

---

you are strange and wonderful
and i hope you find a love
that matches what you are

part one.

there are parts you'll never show
parts of you they'll never know
there's madness in your soul
but you smile through it
laughing at bad jokes
in an attempt to get through it
trying to find peace
but you often lose it

they claim to love you
but they'll never prove it
and moving on is difficult
easier said than done
until you do it

you're surprised
by how strong
you are
but I'm not, you're magic
and I always knew it

part two.

you danced in circles
you danced in the darkness
re-creating the midnight moon
and soon your shade
will become light
and at the same time
every morning you'll rise
like that tremendous big orb of light
you survive, and you shine
you fall, then get back up
you thrive

part three.

tell me the secrets
you've buried
show me the memories
you struggle to forget
tell me your regrets
show me what is hidden
no matter how difficult it gets

i want to see your misery
don't be ashamed
of what haunts you

the only way to defeat your devils
is to confront them
and you can do this on your own
or we can do this shit together

i'd gladly weather any storm
that comes for you
turn your loneliness into us
i'm not afraid of your demons
and i'll stay
because i love you that much

part four.

tainted love fades
just like shade
when the sun rises

a new day could be
your chance to find your strength
or it could be
another moment of misery
as you struggle to walk away
from all the things
that no longer bring you joy

what will the morning bring you
is it happiness, will it be painful
will you survive
or will it be too much

tainted love fades
but the love you give unto yourself
will always be more than enough
to get you through the heartache

part five.

i hope you're doing better
the letters stopped
you're not reaching out anymore
you've gone silent on me
and i can't help but worry about you

i hope these words find you
in your moment of need
and even though you may feel invisible
i hope this helps you feel seen

I hope you see how beautiful it is to begin again without the person you thought you needed.

You carry him and all of his bullshit, but tell me, who carries you when you are too broken to go on?

Not everyone leaves—just the ones who were never worthy of being by your side.

Love yourself entirely, and stay away from anyone who loves you less than that.

---

he offered her the stars
in exchange for her moon
and she said no

I believe it hurts because you spent so much time making plans. You invested so much time while they were busy wasting it without you knowing.

---

a man in love
is motivated
to make sure
the one he loves
feels secure
in their relationship

---

plot twist, she was better without him

Sometimes your emotions are based on lies, and you fall for someone who only intended to break your heart. Don't trust everything you feel. Take your time and know the difference between someone making promises and someone carrying out all the things they've proclaimed.

---

when you're truly in love

your soul will smile and not feel weary

I could already hear it in your voice, and you whispered, "I'm fine." All the while you were falling apart. They don't understand you, and you don't need them to in order to be happy. All that matters is that you are strong enough to feel whatever it is that lives within you, and that's how I know you'll be strong enough to survive. Keep going.

destroy some bridges.

I think it's okay to distance yourself from people who keep you from feeling all the right things. It's essential to make room for more moments that grant the heart the opportunity to feel loved and cherished. You cheapen your life by allowing your heart to be invested in people who break it. Sometimes it's not even a romantic relationship. Sometimes the person you need to break up with is a family member, maybe a close friend. You are never obligated to stay where your heart is unable to thrive. No matter the title that person holds in your life, no one should be allowed to break you down.

---

she cried

but this time

her tears

drowned away everything

that didn't belong

---

not all light is beautiful
you see, some light is blinding
in a way that keeps you
from seeing the entire truth

---

you were never needy
you weren't asking
for too much
you demanded
what was necessary
for you to feel loved
and they were incapable
of meeting those demands

---

ignore them
let them go
focus on your ph levels
drink more water
build your savings account
say no to everything
you don't want to do
do any and everything
that involves you
moving past their bullshit
because you are worth so much more
why stay in a relationship
in which you feel stuck
that's not how you grow

---

so much of the pain
lives in the unspoken spaces
of the heart
moments wrapped in silence
out of fear of being judged

you've hidden so much
of yourself there
where no one sees
until now, until this very moment

don't be ashamed of what you feel
your pain is a part of your story
tell it without fear

There's always that one person who you feel like you can never give up on, and the fucked-up part about this feeling is that person has always given up on you so quickly.

---

you need not unfold your heart
for anyone who isn't willing
to prove themselves worthy
of being loved by you

Someone who takes risks to keep you, not lose you.

---

the love you deserve
is far from ordinary
it doesn't hurt
it won't break you
don't settle

not weak.

First of all, you're not weak for staying. What you need to know is that it takes a great deal of strength to withstand the storm that is heartbreak. It takes a great deal of strength to hold on to a relationship that does nothing but destroy you, but that same power can be used to set you free.

I tell people to move on, and their response is often, "It's easier said than done," and though it's true, I also think it's just something people say to justify their choice to stay with someone who had already given up on them a long time ago. Sadly, you've gotten to a point where instead of fighting for your peace of mind, you'd rather stay with someone who treats you like a piece of shit, and I'm just one person who wants you to remember that you will survive without that person.

You think it's so hard to walk away, but imagine how hard it should be to give all of your love to someone who will never deserve you.

It's time to love yourself enough to walk away. It's time to love yourself so much that you no longer allow others the opportunity to hurt you. I need you to know that you are worth so much more than the relationship you've settled for. I need you to see who you've always been instead of the brokenness they've made you feel. You are more than the pain that resides in your heart.

I know I sound like a broken record, but I refuse to give up on you. Sure, you can hate me, get angry with me, or ignore these messages, but I'll always be here for whenever you wish to listen, to read, to consume these words. I want you to be happy, because you deserve to have peace.

honor and devotion.

Before you could ever be faithful to someone, you must practice loyalty and love toward yourself. What I mean by this is that you respect yourself enough not to put your heart, mind, and body at risk. To cheat would be the destruction of self. Cheating is a confessional act of someone too weak to devote themselves to someone else. Cheating is an admission of insecurity.

My heart can't wander because it's invested in someone I genuinely care about. My eyes can't wander because my partner is the only light I wish to see. My body can't wander because my partner is more than enough in the space of comfort and desire. Most men will have you believe that cheating is a part of our DNA, but if anything, cheating is a disease.

So if you've ever been cheated on, first, be grateful that your partner revealed themselves to you as a coward, and second, stay away from those who are unfaithful to your ideas of love and commitment. It is not your fault, and it is not your job to provide an incentive to someone who isn't strong enough to be faithful to you.

I feel strongly about commitment, honesty, and devotion. If you're incapable of all of the above, leave. Cheating is the game of the weak. A game that the strong need not entertain.

meet the Kings.

i know the ugliness of this world
i've felt it in the way my wife's family
pretended to give a fuck about me
i've seen it in their eyes
their gaze staring upon me
thinking of ways
that they can use me or use us

i've seen the color green
on the surface of their intentions
the jealousy in the voices
as they judge me and my wife
for wanting more for ourselves
more than they could ever have

i think my wife's father
blames me for the fracture
in their foundation
and maybe my presence
woke her soul to the disappointment
that has always lived there

but i assure you that i tried
i made an effort, i gave support
i did and continue to do
what others won't
and for that, those relationships
have fallen apart

i've seen the ugliness of this world
and i've seen so much of it
in my wife's family, my family

for yourself.

you moved the rain
you may not have realized it
but you walked toward me
and the closer you got
it stopped storming

and i guess i just want you
to know your power
to realize your magic
and to use that ability
on yourself, for yourself

part six.

Your fear of love began years ago—the absence of a father, a mother's neglect, and even with the odds stacked against you. Nothing could stand in your way of becoming more than they could teach you to be. And you continue to fight for everything you deserve, and I want you to know that I am proud of you.

She moves like a brush to a canvas, a living art form—a profound expression of resistance as she not only fights for what she deserves, she fights against this idea that she should settle. She moves like lightning in search of a space to land. And you either meet her demands or watch her drift away like a dream in the softness of morning.

---

more self-love

even on your worst days

it's difficult to try for yourself

when you feel broken up inside

but you're learning to continue to fight

---

there is no light on this earth
that could ever compare to yours
you are a rarity, a sight to be seen
a force to be respected
with a love that should be cherished
don't let them make you feel small
when you were born to be great

Some of you reading this are not in search of a love that isn't your own, and what I mean by this is that you're simply looking for more of yourself. You're trying to find true love in the details of your existence, and though you fully deserve to be loved by someone, the most essential romance is the one you experience when alone, on your own.

They will envy you, even while concealing their jealousy. They will look to befriend you, because the enemy wants to be up close to witness your downfall and to judge you for all of your mistakes personally.

The closer you get to certain people, the further you are from everything you truly deserve. Your life and the details of your future can often be altered by the people you spend the most time on.

It's not that you don't care or that you don't have a heart. You're just good at pretending that it doesn't matter even when it's all you ever think about.

We were warned about strangers and the destruction they cause, but no one told us that most of the pain would come from the people who know us, the people who claim to love us the most. And this is a lesson you learn very early in life—that you must be careful with strangers but even more careful with family and friends.

To find balance, you must find a space that isn't occupied by the people who take from you and never give.

Self-care is saying no to people who don't.
necessarily deserve a yes.

Peace thrives in the absence of certain people. Rejoice when the wrong people walk out of your life.

The ending of any relationship can be difficult, but the fact that it's finally over gives you a greater opportunity to love everything about yourself that they didn't.

---

chaos is a distraction

a detour from joy

a destroyer of peace

Do not allow your heart to remain in places it won't thrive.

Start telling the truth about family who lie to you and lie on you.

Your kindness was never a weakness. You were just kind to weak people.

Say no to things that will keep you from living the life you always wanted.

You have always been more than enough, but you have always wanted to be accepted by people who will never be good enough for you. That's the problem. Searching for validation in people who are too stupid to comprehend all that you are.

You have to be willing to walk away from anyone who restricts you from living your best life. This includes family.

A broken woman is a tapestry of strength. The power to conquer and survive are woven beneath her bones and inside her heart and are embedded in her soul.

Phenomenal women are forged in the fires of heartache. And this is how I know that you'll be fine. You feel pain now, but you'll be stronger later. Keep fighting.

---

you feel broken
you feel discouraged
you feel sadness
throughout your bones
but you are still more
and you are still magic

---

a love

rooted in devotion

will grow and bloom

and will not wilt

---

the ocean spends its life
reaching for the shoreline
no matter the distance
no matter the weather
and this is the way love
should be

---

if the night sky were absent of stars
and the lights from tall buildings ceased
you'd still find your way home
because you, my dear, are the moon

---

it's tough

but she's learning

how to be alone

she's learning to find balance

in solitude

---

some days you feel like love
in the spring
and then you turn cold
like the roots midwinter

---

reduced to strangers
because you could never see
the value in my presence
reduced to shadows
that no longer intertwine

Self-care is ignoring their calls. Self-care is no longer listening to their lies.

---

she stared into that broken mirror

with a smile laced in tears

because for once

she could truly see herself

for how she felt

---

i think she stopped looking
to the night sky
when she realized
that she was the moon
and that meant
that she could survive
the midnight hour

---

the mind says, “fuck you”

but the heart whispers, “i miss you”

---

if you don't choose her now
you can't choose her later
if you don't love her now
she'll choose herself
and give unto herself
everything you couldn't
and she will find
the delight in your absence

The sadness chases you down at a relatively young age, and you're left to make sense of something that won't make sense to you because you're too young to understand that the pain of loving the wrong person is temporary and the end of one relationship isn't the end of the world.

too late.

please don't fall in love
with anyone who makes you feel
like the love you deserve
is too much to ask for

---

the first to abandon your heart
is also the one who promised
they'd never walk away from you

again, too late.

please don't go back
to anyone who never intended
to give you a reason to stay

stay, please.

One of my readers wrote me a direct message, and in that message, she explained the pain in her heart, and she asked me not to judge her or to hate her for giving up. I was too late because the following message was a goodbye, and I want her to know that I could never judge her or hate her. I could only have hoped that I could've helped a bit more, and I know that, deep down, she just wanted to escape.

And so, I say this to you, the reader of these words: please stay and allow me to help. Please stay and let life get better. Please stay, because your light is essential, and someone needs it to guide their soul through the darkness you've known. Your light shines so brightly, and it has always been enough to lead you toward salvation. Please stay, because my heart can't take losing someone as mighty as you.

---

you're damaged
fucked up and broken
but you still deserve a love
that reminds you
that your flaws and imperfections
are what make you lovable

---

it will never go back

to the way it was

and you will forever be changed

and though this transformation hurts

you will be stronger than you've ever been

so let yourself evolve

---

stop trying to convince your heart
that it is better off with the one person
who will never know what to do with it

stop trying to convince yourself
that staying and trying harder
will improve a relationship
that isn't meant to get better

Sometimes guys don't even want the person they broke down. It's a hard truth to comprehend, but sometimes a guy wants to prove that he can control someone's heart. And so, for those of you who wonder how he could hurt you while proclaiming to love you, this is how, and someone is reading this now who needed this message. Be strong and choose yourself. It's going to take some time, but you are strong enough to get through this.

Do not build your forever upon the promises of someone who was just searching for a moment.

---

your heart belongs to you
and this is where it should stay
until you find someone
who loves you in a way
that reminds you to love yourself

---

you fall out of love
you fall out of friendships
you fall out of a lifestyle
that is unbecoming
of who you wish to be
you fall out of everything
that no longer fits
your idea of peace and joy
and that is okay
it is okay to fall out of spaces
you can't thrive in

---

don't underestimate the love
of a woman who knows
far too well how it feels
to be broken

You get so wrapped up in how it ends that you miss every opportunity to realize the beauty in beginning again by yourself.

---

saying sorry
does not shake the fear
nor does it remove
the scars of anguish

an apology
does not end
the suffering
in the mind

One day he'll look back to where he broke you, and you will be gone because you decided not to stay there.

---

nearly dammed and damaged
she used whatever she had left
to be whatever it was she needs
in order to survive again

---

how the rain feels
when it finds a place
to land
give me that feeling

---

when your heart is aching
you learn that silence
can be a language

---

you've had all types of love

except the one that stays

---

cry an ocean
create a way
to swim away
from him

---

you’re going to be fine
you were built
for this type of breaking

---

the thing about drowning
is that you find yourself
reaching for help
from the person
who pushed you in
and held your head under water

---

eventually their absence
won't make you miss them
their absence will show you
that there is life
without them

---

she could have anyone

she wanted

and she chose herself

Brokenness is a thing you feel, but it doesn't have to be your identity.

When you search for true love, peace, and devotion, begin with yourself.

Everyone has baggage. Pack lighter next time.

You have a password for everything except your heart and mind.

---

you are a thrill to be with
don't waste your time
being in a mediocre relationship
settling for a mediocre love

---

scars are stories

not always of horror

some are of survival and triumph

---

it hurts

but you're still here

you'll make it

you won

not easy.

The phrase "it's easier said than done" will never be a good enough reason to justify being in a relationship with someone who treats you like shit.

Yeah, I get it. Moving on is hard, but don't act like being with the wrong person is easy. You're either going to stay and remain stuck or go and begin to grow.

You keep saying moving on isn't easy, as if staying with someone who treats you like shit is any easier. I just wish you'd begin loving yourself more than you love the one person who will never love you back.

Remember who you were before the heartache began. Remember how it felt before they entered your life. Sure, you were lonely at times, but here you are, all alone, even as they lie beside you. The love was never real, but you cling to them as if something will change. Believing flowers can grow in a garden with tainted soil.

---

fuck it

you tried

you fought

it hurt

move on

You have to stop chasing behind people who choose to run from you instead of walk beside you. It's time to take everything you have left and give it to yourself. You have to stop forcing people to see something in you they never will.

---

be with someone
who is as loyal to you
as your shadow

---

whatever you'll need

you can get it from yourself

You've been feeling the weight of disappointment for most of your life, and I believe that it is time to let go of all the people who continue to let you down. I get it, you're strong, and you've built up a tolerance for pain, but that doesn't mean you deserve to be hurt repeatedly. Just because you can handle it doesn't mean you should put up with it.

You can take all of your loneliest nights and place them next to an evening in bed with someone who hurts you and none of those nights would even compare to the emptiness you feel whenever you share your bed with the wrong person.

You know those moments when you doubt that they'll ever change? The confusion of it all? The fear of starting over and the pain you feel every time you think of your future and the uncertainty of being with that person? Don't ignore it; don't ignore the questions that fill up your heart in the middle of the night when you can't sleep. I promise you, the answer you've been searching for has been with you all along. You know what you have to do.

---

my wife's big brother
seems so small
the way he never holds
himself accountable
for being absent
from the moments
that really matter

---

there is something in the wind
whispering her name
the wild calls out to her
"free yourself," is what it says

---

all the silence in her heart screams

---

she fixed it on her own

she was the savior of her life

---

be the best thing to ever happen to your own heart

---

end it

then start over

with all the lessons you've learned

---

what is fire
without a woman
holding it

a meaningless flame
destined to burn out

---

winter reaches for her soul

a girl gone cold

rare in ways.

You have always known you were different, but you have always struggled to find the words to explain what it is you have seen in yourself. Your strength unmatched, your will to keep going, despite whatever sadness you've felt, is something that could inspire others. See, you've inspired me to write these words and piece them together like puzzles to create a picture of you—an image with warrior-like features and the demeanor of a Queen. You have always known you were different, and I've also come to know the same.

part seven.

I think your intentions are good. You don't want to feel like you're giving up, but in your pursuit to prove your love, you are hurting yourself, and I don't think that's fair. Especially after you've made the effort you've made. It's important to understand that love isn't something you can force. You can't find real love while entertaining fraudulent people. You'll never truly be happy holding on to those who hurt you.

part eight.

What is love if it feels like hatred? What are promises when they often feel empty? What is trust when the person you believe in betrays you? What is an apology when they're not willing to refrain from the actions they apologize for? The liar lies, the cheater cheats, and more times than not, they say "sorry" without any intention of changing their behavior. I hope you realize this and do whatever it is you need to do with this knowledge.

Some breakups involve family. Sometimes you have to move on from the people you thought you needed, especially when they do nothing but keep you further from peace.

part nine.

It's hard, but you're learning to detach from people who show, time and time again, that they are nothing special. You're learning to put distance between yourself and the people who would rather destroy your self-esteem than build you up. That's a lonely place to be; trust me, I know. But your future will illuminate the moment you walk away, and your life's fire will burn brighter as you continue to let go of everything and everyone who doesn't deserve to be kept. I want you to be happy, but more than anything, I want you to know that true happiness is something you can cultivate and maintain on your own. And once you've done this, you'll be able to share that joy with the person who is willing and ready to prove that they deserve to share in your peace of mind.

artwork.

With strokes of madness on a canvas, she made pain look like art. The way she moved like the hand of an artist in search of somewhere to land. An assortment of decisions, both good and bad, stitched together like pages to the spine of a book. She's abstract because she's not afraid to be. Free and wild, filled with magic in a world that will often be incapable of comprehending the meaning of why she exists. Framed like the masterpiece she is, she could live in museums for all the world to admire. She could go anywhere in the world if she'd like, and cities of people would stop to pay homage to her warrior-like presence. Yes, she could take her aura and shine it in the middle of the night and make the dark skies feel like morning. She could be doing anything in the world, anything she wants, but she's here at this moment. She is reading this book, consuming these words. She is you.

reflections.

Look in the mirror and tell the woman you see that you are proud of everything she has done. Make a promise to be kinder to her. Look her dead in the eye and promise her that you will live your life loving her with all that you have.

So many dreams are painted with lies. They're soft in the beginning, but once you fall, you end up landing on a surface made of stone. You tell yourself that things will change, but the only thing made different are your lips, as you have lost your smile. You begin to break beneath the heaviness of empty promises. You begin to ache in places unimaginable. Your entire future rendered uncertain by the fraudulent character of someone who pretended to love you. This entire event has left you drained, and yet you are full of a form of wisdom that can only reside within the mind and heart of someone who knows what it means to love the wrong person. You learn how to navigate those little fires caused by those who only intend to deceive you. Most times, getting burned is also learning how to survive the flames.

Sometimes I worry about you. Claiming to be okay, saying "I'm fine" even when your whole world is burning down. You stand when falling should be the only option, should lie awake at night even when your heart needs to rest. You move on, you move forward as your legs begin to ache. Searching for everything you lost while loving someone who decided to hurt you. There are nights when I worry about you; there are nights when you fight off the urge to give in, to give up. There are nights when you just feel like the darkness is too much and the light from the moon is not enough, and still you awake the next morning. Full of strength and hope, despite the hopelessness that follows you and the exhaustion you feel for trying to be good enough for someone who was never good enough for you. I worry about you, and yet something within me believes in you and your ability to cultivate whatever it is you need in order to survive.

The world will always need someone like you. Someone who can show it that, no matter how broken the heart may feel, there is a way to keep going. There is a way to stay alive. You are proof that, no matter what ends, there's a way to begin again.

I've been thinking about you and everything you've faced up until this moment. You are proof of warriors walking the earth disguised as everyday people. You may be a civilian, but most days you find yourself at war with many things, and those things find difficulty in trying to defeat you. Yes, there are moments when you fall, there are moments when you feel like giving up; but instead of giving in, you continue to pick yourself up in preparation for victory. And this is how I know you'll be fine. This is how I know you'll make it, because you always do. You always will. And this is what I think about whenever I think of you.

---

she whispered and the earth shook

this is the power of a woman

forgiveness does not mean “come back”

The good memories are excuses to stay, and lately you've found yourself struggling to remember those moments. Your body is beginning to give in to the exhaustion of fighting to love someone who treats you like the enemy. Your feet, once hesitant to move, are now preparing for the tough journey of walking away from someone you thought you could never leave. Here you are, reading these words, a sign of what's to come. A representation of what you've been feeling. Here you are, in this moment, growing closer to the idea of letting go.

another goodbye.

You're lost, and you've been searching for yourself for so long. You chose to pick up this book in search of a sign. Maybe you were hoping for some solace, a vacation from the pain you've felt. Perhaps the words in this book triggered a memory, and perhaps you're still trying to remember who you are and what you are capable of in the aftermath of heartbreak.

For whatever reason, my words ended up in your hands and your heart. I hope you figure out how to piece yourself back together again. I hope you find new ways to survive once more and set yourself free from all the pain that has taken up space in your life. I can't promise to have all the answers, but I do know that the most profound answer to everything you've been asking lives within you. You are the hero in this story, you have always been, and I am just the writer who gets the opportunity to remind you of the magic that dwells within all that you are. Please don't give up on yourself. You're so much more than what you may know. And I hope this was a step further in reminding you that the best is yet to come. Take care. Until next time.

index

#.

8/22/19. 163

a.

A broken woman is a tapestry of strength. 331

a concern of mine. 17

A family is just a group of titles until the individuals in your family give more meaning to their roles by showing up when the time comes. 258

After you've been hurt, everything then becomes "too good to be true." 96

again, too late. 348

All of everything you've ever given was always more than enough. 261

all the silence in her heart screams 387

a love 334

always this powerful. 20

a man in love 290

an abundance of self-respect 14

and i once thought 193

and sometimes she hides 109

And that's why we stay longer than we should, because it hurts to watch something you love transform into something you should hate, something that hurts your heart and soul. 128

and that's your problem 132

and to think 54

And you're just trying to be the only one they'll ever love. 45

And you were broken just as much I was. 240

anger based. 135

another goodbye. 400

answer below. 227

artwork. 398

b.

be careful who you build 243

Because women don't always know that men often send those same texts to several women at a time, it's almost as if they go fishing with lies as their bait, hoping to get a bite. 79

be empty 147

be here now 1

Be kinder to the woman crying back at you in the mirror. 212

be the best thing to ever happen to your own heart 389

be with someone 380

be with someone who moves you 69

beyond the fourth wall. 74

be your own companion 221

Blood may be thicker than water, but it will never be more important than peace of mind and joy within the heart. 257

broken girls 219

Brokenness is a thing you feel, but it doesn't have to be your identity. 370

burn some bridges 120

But isn't that the problem? 85

but you're trying to give your heart 49

c.

chaos is a distraction 324

Choosing yourself means deciding to be happy, despite your feelings for the wrong person. 202

coldest summer. 33

Consider that this life we lead is entirely too short, made shorter by the time we spend on people who were never worth our energy. 256

Correct me if I'm wrong, but I think it hurts because you genuinely give a fuck. 143

cry an ocean 365

d.

Dear woman, 237

definitively you. 197

Despite the change in the weather, despite the storm, she went on growing, blooming, and becoming more of everything she was meant to be. 217

destroy some bridges. 295

Do not allow your heart to remain in places it won't thrive. 325

Do not build your forever upon the promises of someone who was just searching for a moment. 354

do not lose who you've been 272

Don't get me wrong, the stars are beautiful; but you, my dear, are more than that. 118

Don't let a day go by without reminding yourself that you are worthy of a love that makes you feel safe. 235

don't underestimate the love 357

Don't you feel lost? 260

don't you need rest 124

dying to live. 28

e.

each scar is a confession of strength and survival 56

end it 390

eventually their absence 368

Everyone has baggage. 372

Everything about him was fictional 38

eyes filled with a wild flame 24

f.

feel what you need to feel 159

Find your fire and burn through everything that no longer fits into your life. 233

forever is fractured by lies and betrayal 150

forgiveness does not mean "come back" 405

for once, she wanted 58

For you, beauty is much more than the surface. 206

for yourself. 310

Fri 8:09pm. 76

fuck it 378

g.

give me a love 105

Give up the person who forced you to give up your smile. 210

Go someplace where you feel free. 187

gracefully 77

h.

happy to be alone 122

Heartbreak will alter the way you feel about relationships, but don't let the pain keep you from discovering the right person to love. 200

he broke her heart 103

he can't love you 160

he is not sorry 3
He knew he wasn't shit when he approached you. 185
he left, and he should stay gone 59
he made you cold 26
he needs to know. 22
he offered her the stars 288
her heart is too pure 57
her soul 156
her tears are full of ghosts 180
he says nothing when he speaks 35
he's been your nightmare 151
He was never a loss. 264
high frequency. 15
Him 95
his absence 36
his ghost lives in her tears 271
honest enough to say i miss you 101
honor and devotion. 307
hourglass. 140
How is it that you feel bad about leaving him, but he never gives a fuck about hurting you? 230
how the rain feels 362

i.

i am a victim of hoping 154
I believe it hurts because you spent so much time making plans. 289
I can't fault you for wanting to walk away from people who fail to respect you, and no, I don't think you should feel bad for distancing yourself from them. 218
I could already hear it in your voice, and you whispered, "I'm fine." 294
i don't think she's cold 104
i don't think the pain 30

I'd rather you fall in love with the parts of me that no one cares to know. 131

if he loved you 183

if the night sky were absent of stars 336

if you don't choose her now 344

if you wait for him 270

ignore them 299

ignore what he said 148

I hope you find someone strong enough to be soft with you and your heart. 43

i hope you see how beautiful it is to begin again without the person you thought you needed. 284

I know I sound I sound like a broken record, but I refuse to give up on you. 306

I know it's hard because you've been hurt so many fucking times, but you are worth finding. 244

i know you wish to hold on 99

I'll say this. 162

"I miss you," she whispered while staring at her reflection. 62

I'm just not who I was before you. 130

I'm not judging you. 196

I'm tired of always being present in your absence. 164

in position. 83

in silence 274

in the end, you realize 16

in the silence. 93

it almost feels as if 186

I thank you when you've done nothing to help. 165

I think it's interesting that after you get your heart broken, your friends suggest that you go out and surround yourself with the same type of people who will hurt your heart. 80

I think she knew she'd have to let go, yet she held on to parts of him that no longer existed. 133

i think she stopped looking 342

I think you need to know that it is entirely okay to detach from members of your family who cause nothing but pain and discomfort in your life. 250

I think you ought to be in love with yourself a little deeper. 172

I think you're more than capable of doing what is necessary. 21

it hurts 376

It hurts because you genuinely give a fuck. 10

it is not up to you to keep an unkept man 23

It just happens. 215

It may not feel like it. 66

it rains, and this is when you know 44

It's about time you started getting the type of love and dedication you've wasted on others. 121

it's been a long time 174

it's been years 50

It's hard not to be loud about the things you genuinely love. 64

it's hard, you know 110

It's like the longer you hold on to the wrong person, the further you are from the type of relationship you feel you deserve. 199

It's not that you don't care or that you don't have a heart. 318

it's tough 337

it will be hard to leave 78

it will never go back 351

it worked for a while 5

I've been thinking about you and everything you've faced up until this moment. 403

I want you to know that, despite the heartache that has always filled your heart, and even though you're used to being hurt, you still deserve a love that doesn't cause you anguish. 214

I wish you could remember how it felt before he entered your life. 249

i wish your father tried harder 138

I wonder if your shadow grows weary of you dragging it into relationships that were never worthy of your presence. 198

j.

July 22, 2019. 73

l.

Life is beautiful when you begin to say no to all the people who were never worthy of a yes. 88

Love is having someone beside you to confront your demons. 129

Love isn't supposed to feel terrible. 188

Love me as if there is no one else you'll ever need or want 90

Love yourself entirely, and stay away from anyone who loves you less than that. 287

lying to herself 29

m.

Make a list of what you want, need, and deserve. 255

many forms of abuse. 2

Maybe the one you're supposed to be with is distracted by the wrong person also. 211

Maybe you don't give a fuck about what I have to say. 253

meet the Kings. 308

midnight was nothing more than 182

more self-love 313

move on 142

my wife's big brother 385

n.

nearly dammed and damaged 361

never mind the summer 192

no one is you 119

not all light is beautiful 297

not easy. 377

Not everyone leaves—just the ones who were never worthy of being by your side. 286

not weak. 305

o.

of course, he'll live without you 102

old friends 242

one day 48

One day he'll look back to where he broke you, and you will be gone because you decided not to stay there. 360

one day you'll make sense 209

p.

pain seals itself in our tears 224

part one. 278

part two. 279

part three. 280

part four. 282

part five. 283

part six. 311

part seven. 394

part eight. 395

part nine. 397

peace dwells within you 246

Peace thrives in the absence of certain people. 322

Perhaps he was never what you needed, and you only believed in him because he was capable of telling you everything you wanted to hear whenever you needed to hear it. 247

Phenomenal women are forged in the fires of heartache. 332

Please don't let him make you feel guilty for wanting to be cherished and loved. 98

plot twist, she was better without him 291

precious wild woman 7

Purge the idea of him from your heart by accepting the fact that he's always been too weak to appreciate your presence. 231

r.

rare in ways. 393

reduced to strangers 339

reflections. 399

remarkable 149

Remind yourself that you deserve better by letting go of the person who doesn't deserve you. 228

Removing people from your life is a symbol of self-respect. 46

replace him with yourself 51

Right now, you wonder if you should stay, and that alone is a sign. 275

s.

Sadly, the world made her feel guilty for wanting to leave a man who could never appreciate her heart. 9

sadness leaves 173

saying no to him 113

saying sorry 359

Say no to things that will keep you from living the life you always wanted. 328

scars are stories 375

scene fifty-two. 194

scene fifty-three. 213

Self-care is ignoring their calls. 340

Self-care is saying no to people who don't necessarily deserve a yes. 321

Self-love is the best practice of affection. 248

self, safe. 136

she built her own wings 106

she could have anyone 369

she cried 296

she dreams of being loved 161

she felt like breaking 115

she fixed it on her own 388

she grew silent 145

she is a museum of wild art 254

she made herself at home 157

she misses him 39

She moves like a brush to a canvas, a living art form—a profound expression of resistance as she not only fights for what she deserves, she fights against this idea that she should settle. 312

she's always thinking 60

she's been through hell 181

she's committed to herself 137

she sounds like music 208

she stared into that broken mirror 341

she still loves him 269

she stopped demanding him 8

she understands the rain 153

she wasn't sad anymore 107

She was tired emotionally, but she had just enough left to move on with her life. 207

she whispered and the earth shook 404

she wore every face but her own 55

single mothers. 6

single mothers II. 18

So many dreams are painted with lies. 407

Some breakups involve family. 396

some days you feel like love 338

Some of you reading this are not in search of a love that isn't your own, and what I mean by this is that you're simply looking for more of yourself. 315

Someone who takes risks to keep you, not lose you. 303

someone you need 152

some silence 276

something about her 114

Something good happening with someone good enough to love me in the way I need. 191

Sometimes guys don't even want the person they broke down. 353

Sometimes I don't want to be human. 190

Sometimes I worry about you. 401

Sometimes people can't comprehend the power of your love until it's taken away from them without an explanation. 171

sometimes the hurt is good 52

sometimes you get better 177

Sometimes your emotions are based on lies, and you fall for someone who only intended to break your heart. 292

some will fall 203

so much of the pain 300

Start telling the truth about family who lie to you and lie on you. 326

stay, please. 349

stop acting like you're weak 68

Stop giving second chances to fools. 19

Stop holding on to what you should have left behind. 222

stop providing your light 84

Stop searching for closure from a man who wasn't even capable of comprehending your worth and love. 89

stop trying to convince your heart 352

strangely familiar. 259

t.

Tell me why you're crying, tell me why you decide to stay where you're not appreciated. 169

that was her magic 108

The closer you get to certain people, the further you are from everything you truly deserve. 317

The ending of any relationship can be difficult, but the fact that it's finally over gives me a greater opportunity to love everything about yourself that they didn't. 323

the first to abandon your heart 347

The good memories are excuses to stay, and lately you've found yourself struggling to remember those moments. 406

The heart is more honest at midnight when it is too tired to lie to itself. 262

the love you deserve 304

The love you imagined is real, just not with him. 266

The lowest version of the man is the one who texts "I miss you" while lying in bed with the woman he left you for. 47

the mind says, "fuck you" 343

the moon 175

the moon knows her name 226

the more you drown 273

the night sky was her canvas 126

the ocean spends its life 335

The only future you have by holding on to the wrong person is a life that will never know what it means to be loved truly. 167

the pain you feel now 204

There are moments when I wish I had a time machine. 166

there is no light on this earth 314

there is something in the wind 386

There's always that one person who you feel like you can never give up on, and the fucked-up part about this feeling is that person has always given up on you so quickly. 301

there were times 125

The right person will feel like home. 11

the saddest eyes i've ever seen 146

The sadness chases you down at a relatively young age, and you're left to make sense of something that won't make sense to you because you're too young to understand that the pain of loving the wrong person is temporary and the end of one relationship isn't the end of the world. 345

The sad truth is that lonely people tend to choose others who will lead them to more loneliness. 265

The same man who was supposed to protect you left you with no shield, no sword, and so you were tasked to fight off the wolves with your bare hands. 87

the sound of rolling thunder 71

the thing about drowning 367

The tiredness in her eyes, in her soul, and in her bones. 42

the verge of. 13

the war and your survival. 139

the way you survive is art 245

The world will always need someone like you. 402

they chase stars 111

they're too focused 31

they were never lovers 239

They will envy you, even while concealing their jealousy. 316

this world 61

To find balance, you must find a space that isn't occupied by the people who take from you and never give. 320

too late. 346

too often you distract yourself 100

Truth is . . . you're going to go through hardship before it gets any easier. 82

u.

Uncertainty has no place in a relationship. 263

w.

wanting him to be the one 123

we could have been great 134

We judge women based on the ratio of ass, hips, and waist. 127

We were warned about strangers and the destruction they cause, but no one told us that most of the pain would come from the people who know us, the people who claim to love us the most. 319

whatever causes the rain 176

whatever you'll need 381

What happens to your dreams when you can't sleep. 236

what is fire 391

What you tolerate is what they'll continue to give. 41

when you begin 144

when you dream of true love 178

when you're truly in love 293

when your heart is aching 363

When you search for true love, peace, and devotion, begin with yourself. 371

where does love really go 32

while other poets wish 252

wild, ember. 72

winter reaches for her soul 392

women are poems 4

y.

You 94

you are allowed 158

you are a needed phenomenon 168

you are a thrill to be with 374

you are a universe 116

you are rain 267

you are strange and wonderful 277

you are worth 112

you are worthy of your love 155

you can reach for others 220

You can take all of your loneliest nights and place them next to an evening in bed with someone who hurts you and none of those nights would even compare to the emptiness you feel whenever you share your bed with the wrong person. 383

You can't keep giving your attention, time, energy, and love to a person who isn't willing to work for those things. 81

You can't lose a man who never deserved to have you. 12

You carry him and all of his bullshit, but tell me, who carries you when you are too broken to go on? 285

you don't win by playing the game 34

you fall out of love 356

You fear being alone, and so you've chosen to be with the one who makes you feel the most lonely. 201

you feel broken 333

you feel sadness 268

You get so wrapped up in how it ends that you miss every opportunity to realize the beauty in beginning again by yourself. 358

You had greatness in you all along. 232

You have always been more than enough, but you have always wanted to be accepted by people who will never be good enough for you. 329

You have a password for everything except your heart and mind. 373

You have to be willing to walk away from anyone who restricts you from living your best life. 330

You have to stop chasing behind people who choose to run from you instead of walk beside you. 379

You know those moments when you doubt that they'll ever change? 384

you lose her trust 70

you love him 184
you need not unfold your heart 302
you need yourself more than you think 53
You never belonged to him. 223
you're afraid 241
You're almost there, just a little bit longer now. 189
you're beautiful 97
You're built for this. 229
you're damaged 350
you're extraordinary 63
you're going to be fine 366
You're so distracted by how it ended that you don't even realize how wonderful it is to begin again on your own. 40
You're trying to fit real feelings into a fraudulent relationship. 225
Your father half-asses everything, but you accept it. 86
your heart belongs to you 355
your heart is broken 67
your ideas of love 27
your intro. v
Your kindness was never a weakness. 327
Your life is a montage of survival and strength. 65
your pain is your candle 117
your reality. 195
Your relationship is shelter, your partner is a home. 91
your soul is unsettled 92
You thought heartache would win, but you survived it. 37
You've been dancing around the truth for so long that you've learned to move willingly with the lies he tells you. 251
You've been feeling the weight of disappointment for most of your life, and I believe that it is time to let go of all the people who continue to let you down. 382
You've been running from yourself lately, afraid of what will happen when you finally catch up. 216

you've had all types of love 364

You've had this terrible feeling living inside your bones, and it's time to listen to what the aches are trying to tell you. 205

you want so many things 179

you wear sadness as a winter coat 238

you were never needy 298

you who made my soul ache 25

You will find everything you've ever needed in the absence of everyone who couldn't appreciate you. 170

You will wake up from this nightmare. 234

she's strong, but she's tired

copyright © 2020 by r.h. Sin. All rights reserved. Printed in China. No part of this book may be used or reproduced in any manner whatsoever without written permission except in the case of reprints in the context of reviews.

Andrews McMeel Publishing
a division of Andrews McMeel Universal
1130 Walnut Street, Kansas City, Missouri 64106
www.andrewsmcmeel.com

20 21 22 23 24 SDB 10 9 8 7 6 5 4 3 2 1

ISBN: 978-1-5248-5828-5

Library of Congress Control Number: 2020930788

Editor: Patty Rice

Art Director/Designer: Diane Marsh

Production Editor: Elizabeth A. Garcia

Production Manager: Cliff Koehler

attention: schools and businesses
Andrews McMeel books are available at quantity discounts with bulk purchase for educational, business, or sales promotional use. For information, please e-mail the Andrews McMeel Publishing Special Sales Department: specialsales@amuniversal.com.